A WAY OF
UPWARDS

C000103258

To Chris

'Splashing a few notes
on a white wall '

RIC HOOL

Love

Ric

MARCH 2014

CinnamonPress

INDEPENDENT INNOVATIVE INTERNATIONAL

Published by Cinnamon Press
Meirion House,
Glan yr afon,
Tanygrisiau
Blaenau Ffestiniog,
Gwynedd, LL41 3SU
www.cinnamonpress.com

The right of Ric Hool to be identified as author of this work has been asserted by her in accordance with the Copyright, Designs and Patent Act, 1988. Copyright © 2014 Ric Hool
ISBN: 978-1-909077-20-1

British Library Cataloguing in Publication Data. A CIP record for this book can be obtained from the British Library.

All rights reserved. No part of this publication may be reproduced, stored in a retrieval system, or transmitted in any form or by any means, electronic, mechanical, photocopying, recording or otherwise without the prior written permission of the publishers. This book may not be lent, hired out, resold or otherwise disposed of by way of trade in any form of binding or cover other than that in which it is published, without the prior consent of the publishers.

Designed and typeset in Palatino by Cinnamon Press
Cover from original artwork 'Wooden People Falling' by easyshuttle © easyshuttle, agency: dreamstime.com
Cover design by Jan Fortune

Printed in Poland

Cinnamon Press is represented in the UK by Inpress Ltd www.inpressbooks.co.uk and in Wales by the Welsh Books Council www.cllc.org.uk

Acknowledgments

Party! first appeared in *Poetry Wales* Vol. 43 No. 3, winter 2011-12.

The United States of Time and *By a Single Leaf* first appeared in *Scintilla 16*, 2012.

A Change of Destination first appeared in *The Rialto* 74, spring 2012.

Remember Me to One, Time and *Fossil* first appeared in *Envoi* issue 160, November 2011.

When I Begin to Say/It's a River first appeared in *Fire* No. 35, 2012.

Thigh-deep In Snow & Thinking Lee Harwood, 7 Miles High and *Infinite Primes* first appeared in *Tears in the Fence* 54.

A Walking Conversation first appeared in *Red Poets* 14, 2008.

A Last Map of Reconstruction first appeared in the anthology *By Grand Central Station We Sat Down and Wept* published by Red Squirrel Press 2010.

Contents

This collection is dedicated to
Colin Burt, Steve Watson, Fiona Owen
and Eileen Dewhurst

A Way of Falling Upwards

A Last Map of Reconstruction

After lines from, By Grand Central Station I Sat Down & Wept

St Ballista's space shot takes its time across no man's land
so you invent stories like hairstyles walking into a ball
past doors of myth; on banana skin floors

An ear hears the veils and mist which rise from sorrow
returned on tales encoded in scrimshaw
sad upon a last leviathan's tooth

I suspect lost worlds and timeslips tremble your mind
tripped on rehearsals spinning through safety nets
gaped in tears and poor repairs

As adobe thoughts turn nomad at the next cantina
a salt song draws cheeks in orders for tequila; for lemons
danced upon the hat of a Mexican memory

A mark left after that which made it has passed
is lonely on your tongue
and young words are fleshless bones of misspelling
and young words are fleshless bones
and young words are fleshless

Time

You are
there
against
dark water
rushed off
a peat hillside
splintered in
runnels

There
stung
in hard rain
against face
and smashed
memory scree

Glove-gripped
against winter's moan
nearly lost
sudden to mist
blown thro heather
crooning
an unborn emptiness

Clashed flanks of timelessness
/ Cadair Idris

Immovable power
the involvement of mist
dressing and undressing vision
distresses thought
reducing the world to an instance

Rock-ragged glimpses
clash understanding
folded in dreams from unseen heavens
through microdot blizzards of moisture

Then the loneliness

The scrape within the skull

Emptiness has nowhere to bleed

Everything

Saturday evening changes everything
even Saturday evening
the moment she becomes a waterfall

The way water is
leaving its effect
but not itself

A matter of lost ends
leapt synapses
deep ocean flashes

draw attention
to what's missing to what's
been lost

Cheap wine
an unwashed glass   light
plays its dirty trick

Saturday evening changes everything

Rigid Smiles

Walking away
beyond distance
stretches every sense

Promises snap
Beliefs snap
Snap goes something
so important
it can't be named

Colours have no
landing stage
                    Butterflies without wings

Painting
a white room white
its window looks down
on tangled trees
broken paths
and
the drowsy night-lit entrance
to a public toilet

                    no one has changed that
bulb for years

Beyond distance
nothing is
close or
far

Remember Me to One

Snow sweeps in like a memory
from a polar direction coldly
on the quickly stupefied valley streets
a Girl of the North Country
casting petticoats and underwear without care
virgin in morning
wasted by evening

Snow sweeps in like a memory in white

The United States of Time

Walking Hills above Llanfairfechan
For Eileen Dewhurst

Ice-block winds
and my head's in
the step of a shoe
towards a stone circle

A metamorphic warrior
beard-long and open mouthed
to day's first sunlight
unwelcomes me

And I'm a step
ahead of a footprint
in winter's shoe

Weather is an agent
of Time building ahead
ready to move swiftly to my present
then past – messenger clouds
scud – pannus

Rent skies
snow-spat purple-grey
and I'm a beggar's coat
against February

Becoming Giant

Sunset will hang in half an hour
above standing ground where   ·
footfalls stop on rock

The body breaks
aches its eating-self-lone-way
chewing muscles over
high ground with ears
stethoscope on each breath

Isn't this the way it is
between us   the years
of tiptoed circles
cut flowers and vases
feeling waiting's weight

On this mountain
thoughts think quickly
escape like prisoners
ravens splitting wings
cracked by cold blasts

Voice-Over

Lights blink in widows over cooling dusk
looking out to the harbour
awash with small craft ferrying small cargo and folk
from jetty to jetty to the jingle of small change

Sampans swish like disturbed insects
on a sea holding the sunset
gold on swells pushed from an oar
to settle behind as fine rolled silk

Three young women giggle in a huddle
faces bent together half hidden by fans
lips reddened for the night and somewhere
ahead the darkening shore

Time loses colour
Windows close as disappearing
houses are swallowed
in the gape of silhouetted hills

A last wish sun snaps shut
Night's tight lid is pressed home
Boats spill their last treasure

Initiation

In Suruga Province waterfowl in flight
watch the world change
Yesterday's map redrawn so urgently
before the reed cutters' blades

Men chatter and call and hack
tracks into the six feet tall beds
towering above their stooped backs
and waded legs

Herons whinge into flight
and small fish fan in silver waves
to deeper darker water

A boy squeals as an eel squirms
between his toes
The men whoop in laughter

Work makes morning afternoon
when castles of waiting reeds halt cutting
to be bundled onto tethered oxen

Weariness closes conversation
and straws are lit to burn off leeches
turgid on legs – the boy squeals again

Each man tows an ox
bushy with thatch to keep the village dry
What water has grown will keep rain out

When night squeezes light to thinness
the reed beds shake back to balance
Webs of life reshape

Summer's Gift

Families work the early morning road
stirring fog that lifts from night-wet ground

Ponies lumped with barter tap tap onward
necks hobbled low by bridle and rope
heads reined in to slow stabbing steps

They have three hours to make
the 7 a.m. market and seven miles to go

Hiromi checks her golden pheasants
They are caged suns rising
as their feathers collect daylight

She has tended them since they hatched
and on the strength of their sale
will buy winter shoes to fight the snows

A sharpening stone is heavy
on the shoulders of Hiromi's father
          landslides heavier on his mind
Dry rocks whisper down slopes

No one talks
Sounds are limited

Hiromi thinks of feet
warm in winter shoes
          smiles into the future

A Change of Destination

The inn on the Tokaido Road has
beautiful ladies that serve refreshing tea
to travellers too exhausted to travel further

In evening there is dancing and music
beneath cherry trees   Sometimes
the blossom falls like fragrant snow

One lady dances with tiny steps
her eyes fireflies
along the horizon of her fan

Later she sits with me without conversation
I tell her my name
stabbing my chest repeating my name

She almost smiles
almost nods her head
is as silent as far off Fuji

I am given tart wine and drink
as if taking communion
then follow her to the ends of the Earth

Rhythms in Orange & Blue

'Oye Como Va' by Tito Puente
For Suzi

At the Café del Mar
music plays down the sun
slipping from the sky
melting into the sea beyond tables set
with glasses rippled in condensation
soaking into paper coasters

The saxophone player bumps octaves
splashing high notes
against a white canvass canopy
shooting golden arrows
back to the drowning star

       Orange & blue
a terracotta roof beneath cobalt sky
a fisherman's burned back against sea

       Original colours

Oye como va mi ritmo
       Dig my rhythm – check my groove

The element fire
The element water

Bueno pa gozar mulata
       Enjoy the mix – the sensual pleasure

The music dreams this realm
tipping the sun to wake another

       My lover takes my hand

How I Met You

That day
lost in low cloud

Mynydd Preseli
captured in cataract-grey

the way gave way
to blindness

Safety
a speck on memory's horizon

the ground
gobbled every step

The ulcer of fear
made nonsense

of map and terrain
they just didn't match

Walking on compass
counting steps

forgetting the count
It was all so going wrong

Falling over
the first stone

I tumbled
into Bedd Arthur

by some act
of chance

this is how
I met you

Old Habits

Collecting mushrooms for Richard Downing

Panthercap next to Stinking Dapperling
angel the forest floor   They challenge
the narrative of return after ingestion

The come back trip is knife-edged
a shimmered darkness   a bat
fluttered in the mind asking
                              Who are you?

The body loses geography
Each organ sniffs in the track of each organ
in a drive towards holism

A moth in flight in iron

The habit of predecessors raking the ground
pawing and bringing to light dark manna
walks through aisles of ancientness

As if dousing candles uneasy to go out
I bend to the forest floor
fingers panning for phallic heads
my pocket guide at hand
ears rung with warning

                    The Sickener
                    Yellow Stainer
                    Death Cap
                    Deceiver

Looking Down

Where no gates close school

      Where fields are not fenced

Where thoughts unwound by razor-wire rejoice

      Where ground-sound informs foot

        its joyous dance says

      All belongs to me that I can see, feel, and be

So how poor is a man? How really badly off?

Arriving this way like falling

      upwards the landscape is full of reasons

erosion working towards balance revealing synclines

      smiling on peaks and looking down

as light is lost road lamps glow

      a luminous henge scribing a roundabout

wound by speeding headlights

These lines of night bring down a walker

      bring a walker down

before darkness devours everything

      and progress made in Braille

When I Begin to Say / It's a River

Long Tailed Tits. Six little runaway acrobats out on fun in the early morning, and each balancing like Charles Blondin over Niagara Falls equalizing round bodies on every perch with their five inch tails

They fall back in military fashion: front bird to furthest perch; second to the perch beyond. So it goes in brief-signalled tweets, almost a grey-pink-cream-white-black mist of movement retreating into branches of silver birch

This is it for about 1 minute. There, in this moment of great beauty – I mean all of it – the day begins its hugeness

Hugeness seen so often in Northumbrian skies zooming out east, west, north, south and taking the eye as far as it can go

clouds making oriental paintings on fine days and big, black gods on others, voicing thunderously at will on the shoulders of a walker coming down from the Simonside Hills, above Rothbury

Ah, the big fire at the pub is salvation and reward

A local begins a tale of the wilds of Wanie (lost pathways around the River Wansbeck) only to dry up as his glass empties

He waggles it in hand making some conjure. Would you believe it? It works! The glass fills: the story tells itself to end and the room is silent, gone to another place

The smell of foxes in first morning and her rich-red hair spilling over pillows, as breathing flexes the room, remembering only what wants to be remembered and thinking how much space can fill a moment

Thinking how much the moment and place are something of a potion, unique and magic enough, never to be made again in perfect likeness

She sits at the dressing table looking into the mirror as if vaguely recognizing her reflection

It does all she does, brushes its wild hair to tameness, lipsticks the curve of the mouth and defines eyelashes, ready again to ambush

Effulgent sunlight reflected from the silvered back of the hairbrush scatters itself about walls and ceiling finding eyes, blinding them for being Peeping Toms

In that place of darkness, in chthonic chambers, inching, squeezing a body thro' nipped tunnels of nightmare, dehiscing lungs, scraping skin, clawing fingernails from sore flesh, is the blanket fear of being alive in a place of deathly hush and has a past life

It explodes in a scream and bursts from the ground, shivering like a silver birch in a spinney of brethren under the fixed stare of the moon, feet rooted in clods of earth, fungi beading and ready, already, to take its body

An idea from a place where birch trees grow, works the currents in a spangling river, which branches where it must, rooting itself to the sea

The language of water

And what parched tongue wants not the word of water

Nothing lasts forever? But
the importance of something might...

Paddling a canoe
pushing water
feeling
water in muscles
grouped
in this feeling

The river
a body of strength
wrestling and at one
both
instantly and continually
as canoe and river independently
and mutually
make progress

There is nothing but importance
in this agreement

The canoe lumbered onto bank
The river vanishes

Driving Forward in Reverse

Life   its burdens   those things
not considered suddenly
make movement
that much harder
that much
                slower

There's been a shift
in my perception
of life since   Why?
This is the question

Suzie Rotello died this week   She
the icon of young love on
The Freewheelin' Bob Dylan album sleeve
She was 19 then   I never met her

Why has she occupied my thoughts
over the years and why should I
by chance hear of her
death on *Radio 4*
switched on
yesterday
in the car?

After The Gold Rush

For Phil & Val Maillard

Evening and how quickly
darkness is about the windows
Summer spins behind
flicking up her skirt
she dances away

In Spain the hell of tourism
is banked and prospects turn
to a kinder time
a time to fall in love

Early morning whispers
brush back sheets
comb back hair
Things are arranged
put in place
no forgets
a few regrets
always untidy ends

                   sadness for what is
and tenderly abandoned

7 Miles High

For Chris Torrance

Often watched Griffon Vultures in Spain. Often watched
them catch a thermal kicked up from the base of an incline
and kite in the mystery of flight to stringlessly let go
leaving land like a memory; leaving land
telescoping away in easy circles, away telescoping
until Scotland and Table Mountain made horizons, until
wings stretched, until
feathers made knowledge
until eyes filled with blue

Heather

Bathing or was it
swimming something says
it was felt

The moment lives in itself
by accident of being and
breathing hillside-honeyed-air

So it is taken
to my writing chair to
fingers searching for
that moment once more

By a Single Leaf

For Chris Hall

Coming down slowly coming down
from last night's heaven
                from last night and feeling holy
coming down

a small

        falling

            leaf

slowly descending

                    dropping as slowly   as it
                                    can
Your heaven
My heaven   so many
heavens

Let hells not be the measure of being
however hard they press and press and bear down
running us scared into corners

Let the wild be wild
and godless of missionaries

Now to stand large
find and lose language

to be open to be

                laid low by a single leaf

In Thanks For Your Love

Thro broken skies
thro alibis
thro a bad joke
an idea
thro opportunity
a phone call
asking

Thro a postcard
thro a dream
thro a headline
a swollen stream
Thro rain
thro the afternoon
thro an ached head
a train
a sickness of roads
by chance
in the weave of it all
you arrive as cloth

In this
I am rapt

Thigh-deep in Snow & Thinking:
Lee Harwood

During a walk in The Black Mountains in deep snow, early January 2010

The drift is 8 feet high and curled
like a surfer's dream wave
I think
they call the shape a tube
and
crawling thro carefully
the whole frozen moment stays intact
perfect
sudden as his verse
unfinished as his lines are completely

Two hours
Two miles
there is no hurry
no misplaced foot
A meditation begins as
breath
          step
                    balance
are things considered and secret

Tracks of wildlife
A dragged-belly kill snakes downhill
swallowed
underground

But how is Brighton?
Wish you were
here   I might just
thud a snowball off your shoulder
just to see you turn
and laugh

If you can

For Kiki

Wake each morning
excited by waking
Bathe in bed-luxury
but swim out

Have knowledge of half-light
and sounds of ebbing night
The nightingale in the ear
is a robin

his chest rising
to the day
his call paving
the way

Say Good day
to cow-shadows in cow fields
to horse-shadows
in horse fields
to shadow itself
and draw it into light

Wag a finger as a wand
Wind it into mist
See   patterns   paintings   possibilities

See a finger
poke itself into day

Wish

For Steephill Jack

Take me with you
in your eyes to Woody Bay
to that wilderness
of sea-scattered detritus

Blink once then see me
head down rustling pebbles
Blink once more
and there I'll be
hard against the sea
as it throws up message
after each far flung message

Reminder

In the arms of a poet
you should know

Sugared salt
Jewelled bread
A stone lion's mouth
Martlemas mutton
A milkmaid's dream
Dancing geese
Maypole flight
Bottomless pools
Blinded sight
Rivers rushing
A given green gown
Memory's pain
Understanding's stupidity
The tears in tears
Colours of Paradise
The blade of words
A second's history
Spade-dug earth
Mountain rain
A search for heaven
Wishing & hoping
A rabbit's ear
Light-lit leaves

Yeah   Yeah   Yeah

Twice-struck lightning
Philosophy dancing
The first picture show
Doc Holiday's last cough
A fabulous fractal object
Infinite zeros
Love's run on empty
Six of one
A boundary-hit ball
Columns
Crystals
Chemical chaos
A formula for failure
Snakes & Ladders
The chance of certainty
A Sermon on The Mount
Half of half of a half of a half
of a half of a half of a half of a
half of a half of a half of a half
never leads to nothing

Infinite primes
Prejudice
Fair play
A rocking horse winning day
The ultimate koan
Every Munro
Forgotten futures

Tell me what I say

You understand
this has no end
my friends

In the arms of a poet
you should know

Harry

My neighbour Harry had guys
to cut down two trees
in his garden that got too tall but
paid up front as he was going out
after the first tree was lumbered

The tree fellers had all the gear
winches ropes karabiners chainsaws
hard-hats and spikes fitted
to the toes of their boots

The outfit had muscle all over it
I watched as the first tree came down
in six   six feet sections
bringing the sky into picture as it did
– the sky so blue

A machine on the ground loudly munched up
the tree parts into chippings
turning that thirty-six foot giant into
a jigsaw of deadness

As said Harry paid then split
to get on with his business.
The tree fellers stopped theirs
the minute he left

The second tree had a second life
standing to this day it gives depth
to the view out of my garden

Harry and I never mention the tree fellers
nor the height to which poplars grow

The remnant slim green column sings soft
in summer and whines in winter
It stands totem to a lamentable work ethic
and a person's misjudged trust
in his fellow man

I Dream of My Mother

My mother joins me on a mountain

I climb ahead
picking out handholds
and ledges to rest on
turning every now and then
to see how she is

And there she is   always
right behind me her face
neither smiling nor sour

Coming round a steep ridge I see
climbers above
first one then another come off
knuckles white around hunks of mountain
suddenly fallen
quickly away

No sound

No screams

I turn to my mother
Are you alright?
She replies
I can't go on
She says
I can't go on

Her face close behind
neither smiling nor sour

Infinite Primes

A January Walk in the Black Mountains with Mikka

The lonely lane to the reservoir winds coldly upwards
past no-one-there farms until
no one there is reality

Hallelujahs and heavens are in the air
striking a ribbon above the valley
slicing cool blueness

Complexity splits common sense ends

       Further

pine tangled paths stepped with
crackle-glass water
break free of the trees to a bald hill ahead
Thickening snow makes
each tread a thrown dice of depth

The path is discarded
as a word of convenience

Invention finds the blasted ridge above
hammering its will against standing
inside infinite primes of being

Three Beads of Morning:

Wren

Hail flamethroatfive a.m. alarm
jail breaking me from a dream
You have a lot to answer for
oh that dream

Out there
beyond the spell of this bedroom
your dynamite song has hushed
the clucking blackbird

Unshakeable
              you are
sure as a leather button
brown as a quartered penny

Awaken

Breathing remembered
a pillow softened
a room beyond the body
examines a window
looks outside

First Light

Morning
the matter unleashed

Darkness
loses its hiding

Each brick
in each east facing wall lit

A legacy of making   colours cooked

Ah breakfast!

Undress Your Coded Exterior

A walk from Freshwater to Yarmouth, April 2009

Boats are washed up ideas
dead on mudflats
skeleton masts and hollow hulls
left to upright in the flood tide to come
for a few remembered hours
all watched over by lonely shorelined benches
dedicated to ghosts

Tightly budded branches sieve sunlight
which clatters through untuned
breaking the ground in a tessera
of angular projections
conducted by the war of batons above

A path constructed on the deconstructed
railway line winds its grey serpent way
sandwiched between mudflats and trees
absurdly ceremonially countryside chic
signing the times and summer walkers
only weeks away

The Poet Falls Out of Love
& Down a Mine Shaft

Hardness replaces grass and leaves
as light surrenders uneasily
its fingers grasping
the descending pit shaft wall

Tunnels echo the changes
as voices lose themselves
in corridors of time

        Darkness gasps
               a ventilation door opens

Dumb tramlines
and melancholia rust

Air and water
in circular motion
make antipodean music

And feel that breeze
               a whisper from the surface

Ear to the Ground

For Lee Harwood

I know that path
Budleigh Salterton along the River
Otter reed beds from 18 years ago   The pebbled beach
kids skimmed stones from towards forever

Your meeting Tzara   I really don't know
much about   The sixties revolution
surely killed off by money by The Beatles'
financial wrangles
until song writing dropped its song but the song
sings it on
          'The eastern world it is exploding'
               Barry McGuire / PF Sloan

A noumenal battle tearing the Earth's plates
phenomenal wars murdering its surface

Moving outward   spaceward   away from
                         autochthonous

Three Views of a Mountain

1

A bud opening

the summit stood in full bloom

2

I am the mountain

kissing clouds & the kiss

between cloud & mountain

3

At the top

there is nowhere else

Way Down Glynmercher

For Chris on his birthday, 24 March 2011

Here's the stop
The place to look down
to watch a few moments dreaming
that different world
ready to be entered

The sign is smoke curling
from the single gable-end chimney
and takes mind to the hearth
to heat
        to Hestia
            to heart

The road is snake-down steep
past stumps of storm-torn trees
beside a stone-rattled stream
before a farm gate opens to a field

The field is open to another – like poetry
March   with spawn-goo puddles
July   soil shrunk to show stones
October   scattered with decay-colour
January   spiked in iced-grass architecture

This and the next field
are trod towards the garden gate
roped against stray sheep

Barricades are built each year and each year
the sheep sense the sweetness
sung in Demeter's breath
which is Glynmercher's garden summer-long

The Perfection of Effort

For John Jones, Graham Hartill & Tim Rossiter

Sun so low and clouds cast themselves
over remnant light   The walk begins
along the velvet path to the south of Sugar Loaf
rising until the incline has breathing like a steam train
The summit approach scrambled over rocks to arrive
at the gusty top   The view over glacial footprints

Descent is westwards   dew-ponds
already frozen over as warmth fades
The sky shafted by the last bolts of sunlight

Stride increases into a valley of quietness
gaining time against oncoming night
then up the opposing valley side by a wet muddy trail   again
to look down upon lights of villages and market towns
Glangrwyney   Llangenny   Crickhowell   I think
of nearby friends   Graham   John   Tim
The last mile walked in darkness lit by them

Crickhowell Bridge: Summer Rain

A bridge and a river in conversation
familiar yet fresh

Huge energy hurtles through conduits
hardly coping with the unexpected forces

New powers extrude finding fresh channels of
tension over many surfaces   The road bridge

liquefied to a vertical fall   falling
into an unseen plunge-pool

Rain sweeps a virginal veil masking landscape
to soft focus   The gentleness of precipitation's

sensual play to the river's outrage   Everything is going
somewhere   moving   bending   re-shaping to a purpose

Fossil

Talking
laughing   slowly
losing your face to darkness
then only
listening
The night pulls itself
over you

On waking
a whirlpool of buzzards
wind up morning
mobbed by ravens of doubt
and further off
like a hawk you quarter
my thoughts

Meanwhile
the elixir of coffee beckons
Its tang
a styptic
to brooding

The kitchen ahead
where you are lion
to my lamb-like entrance
Then your smile
dissolves an acorn of uncertainty

Meanwhile
impressions forgotten in time
blink in the light of discovery

The Frog Murderer

It happens
it happens   Why
should I be
a special case?

For a few weeks a few
sunrisenneversettingforsythiabloomed
weeks   allurement spawned
kicked into a thousand wriggles
thrilled   giggled   grew
hopped   jumped   leapt
                                    sometimes
from stomach to throat

Then stopped

They say conditions
must be right
for things to flourish

                    That so
it's what to do?   And the weight
of one thousand dead frogs

Simple Poem

For Peg

You smile
laugh so much
your face
forgets itself

Your hand warm
makes mine with yours
holding hands

I look up from my book

you smile
your face forgets

your hand warm

Blondes and Motorbikes

For Eileen

They've done something to Talisker
Would be if you got poem-stuck a sip
would be Muse piss would be
October's high tide
force of which glyphs on impact
rock-writ and dragged back exhausted

I have little interest in young blondes
no interest in motorcycles
My life is adventure
that multiform possibility
wave ready to travel then crash

Does that sound like
me
      a blonde
          a motorbike?

      Perhaps

Party!

In a room of voices beating all four walls
town-talking best secrets out
exchanging violin and idea   The Hot Club of Paris
making the most of a moment
There is no escaping this word stew
everyone so spiced and Jeff always
adding too much chilli sends the temperature soaring
                    Who'd have thought Tom
would get into The Ballad of Jamie Allan? Perhaps
there were pints of beer in it to chase off
the glass dagger draughts that stab his flat
in the dead cold of an Alston winter
                    And Hilary sad eyed and skin
needing two weeks in Spain straddles over the hurdle
separating haute couture and being a home girl is losing
weight   lots of it and is energized by the attention
she gets   why not? She has been quiet and plump
too long   so long to the spritzer I see she has
champagne
                    The air is trafficked with stories
Pretty soon there'll be gridlock   worse a crash
with no survivors to tell of how all these people
shoehorned into this room arrived from fallout
or migration or just fluke
                    As if in a western diaries are drawn
He can't do Monday and she can't Thursday so
the moment's heat is lost to the cost of organization
the affair nipped   the briefest encounter
          There is talk of Easter Island and Summer Isles
stone heads and Wicca from wizards posing as scientists
cautiously setting up an old fashioned orgy
                    for the following weekend
There's nothing wrong with nudity says an invisible man
to a newly clothed emperor who flutters
                    to a more fragrant bloom

A cat springs on the table
licks the sardines out of the sandwiches
The coats on the next room bed move rhythmically
The toilet queue becomes conga along the landing
Everyone drinks someone else's drink   apologetically
It's good to have a laugh says the executioner
to the comedian who at last sees irony
as his ultimate enemy

The Only Way is Up

This is a snapshot of steps
cut into a clay cliff above
a pebble beach on the west
coast of an island during summer

Driftwood has been collected and pegged
as risers to give the treads support
and pebbles fetched and emptied
 into each horizontal against wear

There is no sign of the cutters
just their work abandoned as if
for some urgency elsewhere
perhaps more steps   another cliff

At the cliff top is a sign painted red
with white writing warning
DANGER   the steps creep right up
behind the sign
DANGER   it seems
only comes from one direction

Boundaries of Infinite Complexity

For Bill Wyatt

6 a.m.
blades of grass
on the cusp of being

frosted

A river of light
from map
to fluid flow

Crepuscular rays
swig mountains
gulp flora as
lenticular clouds
spaceship northern
skies

NOTHING & EVERYTHING

It falls to
the sure sound

breathing

heartbeat

breathing

heartbeat

breathing

heartbeat

A Walking Conversation

In life
out of systems
a nobody in a place nobody
is near
letting the spirit loose
unrestricted
upon land that teaches
all that cannot be learned
elsewhere

Becoming a part of land
with feet grown in inclines
sunk in mire
drowned in water
making sure decisions
upon the way

If I said
anything else
this is
what is
most important